People of the Ice

People of the Ice

How the Inuit Lived

Heather Smith Siska

Illustrations by Ian Bateson

Douglas & McIntyre
Vancouver / Toronto

For Evelyn: The spirit of *CCM* lives on

Special thanks to Alistair Macduff,
Gallery of the Arctic, Victoria

Copyright © Heather Smith Siska, 1980
Illustrations copyright © Ian Bateson, 1980

First paperbound edition, 1983

Douglas & McIntyre Ltd.
1615 Venables Street
Vancouver, British Columbia

Canadian Cataloguing in Publication Data

Siska, Heather Smith, 1941-
   People of the ice

   ISBN 0-88894-287-7 (bound) —
   ISBN 0-88894-404-7 (pbk.)

   1. Inuit — Juvenile literature.*   I. Bateson,
Ian.   II. Title.
E99-E7S57   j970'.00497   C80-091196-2

Typesetting by Frebo Studio Limited
Jacket art and book design by Ian Bateson
Printed and bound in Canada

Contents

INUIT TRIBES

1 Nunivak
2 Bering Sea
3 North Alaskan
4 Nunamiut
5 Mackenzie
6 Copper
7 Caribou
8 Netsilik
9 Iglulik
10 Baffin
11 Polar
12 East Greenland
13 West Greenland
14 Ungava
15 Labrador

 Areas once inhabited

.... Today's northern and
southern extremes of
habitation

Bering Sea

3

4

1 2 ALASKA 5

11 GREENLA

6 8 9 10

7

14

Pacific Ocean CANADA

USA

The Land

13

tlantic Ocean

15

The frozen land of the Canadian Arctic stretches north of the treeline across the top of North America from Alaska to Greenland. Here, for more than four thousand years, have lived the people of the ice, the Inuit.

For about nine months of the year the Arctic is a windswept polar desert covered in snow. The soil is always frozen just below the surface, and in winter the seas turn to ice. The climate is one of the harshest on earth.

But the Arctic is very beautiful and full of variety. In the far north, surrounded by massive icebergs, are mountainous islands cut with deep fjords, snowfields and glaciers. Farther south is the vast rolling plain known as the Barren Grounds, the treeless tundra. The west is low-lying, with small bluffs and cone-shaped, ice-cored hills called pingos. Areas to the east are rough and rugged. Some gravel beaches extend inland several miles. All across the Arctic, low-lying areas are mostly muskeg, a wet, spongy bog formed by layers of decaying vegetation. Higher ground is often covered with stones squeezed upward by the constant freezing and thawing of the earth.

The Arctic winter is long and cold, the summer short and cool. In midwinter there is almost no daylight, but the northern lights — the aurora borealis — lighten the dark skies with curtains of colour. In midsummer there is no darkness at all.

Some parts of the north get less rainfall than the Sahara Desert. But when the snow melts in summer and the water cannot drain into the earth because of the permafrost, a maze of streams and ponds is

1 Saxifrage	7 Tree sparrow	15 Arctic char
2 Lichen ("caribou moss")	8 Whistling swan	16 Caribou
3 Arctic poppy	9 Rock ptarmigan	17 Musk ox
4 Arctic cotton (used for lamp wicks)	10 Harlequin duck	18 Arctic ground squirrel
5 Arctic snowy owl	11 Narwhal	19 Arctic hare
6 Crow	12 Beluga whale	20 Tundra wolf
	13 Walrus	
	14 Ringed seal	

formed. Here grow over 2,500 kinds of lichens, 500 different mosses and 900 species of shallow-rooted, flowering plants.

Summer is brief but bursting with life. Birds and insects fill the air, animals awaken from hibernation and spiders and beetles scurry across the ground. The white landscape changes to brown and grey, dotted here and there with splashes of yellow, purple, orange, green and red, from poppies, saxifrage, heather, camomile, lupines, mosses and lichens.

Plants take centuries to grow, for in the north only a few inches of earth ever thaw, and the growing season is sometimes only forty days. Lichens may grow only 1 centimetre (⅜ inch) in 1,000 years. Farther south, the soil may thaw to a depth of several feet during a three-month growing season, but even then a 400-year-old willow branch is often thinner than a man's thumb.

In the North of long ago, whales, narwhals, seals, walruses, caribou, bears, wolves, wolverines, hares, foxes, ground squirrels and musk oxen were plentiful. The seas and rivers were full of salmon, trout, Arctic char and cod. Bird life included ducks, geese, ptarmigans, guillemots, terns, murres, golden plovers, snowy owls, horned larks, snow buntings, swans, sparrows, falcons and ravens.

The people of the ice did not try to master the land but to adapt to it. They took from the land only what they needed to survive.

The People

Until recently, the people of the ice were known as Eskimos, from an Indian word meaning "eaters of raw meat." But they prefer their own name, Inuit, "the people."

The Inuit are believed to have come to North America from Asia. They belong to the Mongoloid race, but are taller and have oval rather than round skulls. Their hair is straight and black, their eyes brown, their cheekbones high and their faces wide. Inuit babies are born with a blue patch at the base of their spines, but this disappears after one or two years.

Areas of initial Inuit settlement

STAGES OF INUIT CULTURE (dates approximate)	
Denbigh People (Alaska)	3000 B.C.
(Canada)	↓
Pre-Dorset	2500 - 800 B.C.
Dorset	700 B.C. - A.D. 1300
Thule	A.D. 1200 - 1700
Present Day	A.D. 1600 +

Portion of an ivory bow drill. The carving shows kayakers approaching a swimming caribou (left), and two umiaks (top edge).

A happy, friendly people, patient and independent, they accepted what life brought them and improvised when it fell short of their needs. Both men and women became master craftspeople.

They were mainly a coastal people, but hunting also took them inland, so they became nomadic. They fished or hunted according to the seasons, the weather and the availability of game.

While men sought food, women prepared hides, sewed, gathered driftwood and cared for the family.

Inuktitut, the Inuit's spoken language, is not related to any other. Although there were not many Inuit and they were scattered over a vast area, their language in the different regions was similar enough that they could understand one another.

In the *Inuktitut* language, words and word roots form complete thoughts. *Igdlo*, a house, can become *igdlorssuaq*, a large house, or *igdlorssualiorpoq*, he builds a large house. So ideas are linked together in one word, like a sentence in other languages.

Before the missionaries arrived in the nineteenth century, the Inuit had no written language, so they carried all their knowledge in their heads. They preserved their history by storytelling. Hunting records were sometimes kept by drawing or carving animal shapes or symbols on a piece of hide or bone. Their calendar divided the year into thirteen periods of twenty-eight days each, according to the moons.

Moving by umiak to summer caribou hunting grounds

Each month described something that happened at that time, such as *Kah-pid-rah* (it is cold), *Hir-ker-maun* (the sun returns), *A-von-eve* (the baby seals are born).

There were not many Inuit, only one person per 400 square kilometres (250 square miles). Because they were so few, their society was not highly organized. They lived in small bands of five to ten families, some of whom were related. In late summer, two or three families hunted caribou together, and in winter, groups of families settled together at the seal hunting grounds. While an individual band might be identified by a specific name, larger groups became known by where and how they lived, for instance, Mackenzie Eskimos, Caribou Eskimos.

The Inuit had no government and no laws as we know them, and everyone was equal. The land and its wealth belonged to all. But there was usually one man in each band (often the best hunter) who was an unofficial leader. He organized the hunt and decided when to move the campsite. Families did not have to follow unless they wanted to. Individuals could look after their own affairs, but matters of importance to the group were decided by the group.

Today there are about 100,000 Inuit in the world, living in northern Alaska, Greenland, the eastern tip of the USSR and northern Canada. The Canadian Inuit population numbers about 23,000. Many of them live like other Canadians and few of their old ways remain. But the Inuit today are proud of their rich heritage.

The Family

The Inuit family included parents, children, grandparents, aunts, uncles and any relatives who did not have a hunter to provide for them. They lived together in one shelter, or in several built closely together.

An Inuit man married as soon as he could hunt food to keep a wife, a woman when she reached puberty. Sometimes couples were promised to one another at birth by their parents. If not, there were no special rules of courtship. Usually a man visited the parents of his chosen bride to find out if her father approved of him. Women had little or no say in the matter. Sometimes a payment might be agreed upon; at other times the groom pretended to "kidnap" his bride. There was no formal marriage ceremony: a couple simply began living together.

Sometimes a man had more than one wife. There was much work to be done, and one woman could not row the large *umiak* when the family was on the move. If a wife was sick and could not travel, a man might borrow a wife from a friend. In the harsh climate of the Arctic a traveller could die if his garments became torn and he did not have a woman to mend them quickly.

Without strength and stamina to hunt for food, the people of the ice would die. Children were especially important to them. Having children — especially sons — meant that a couple would have someone to look after them when they grew old and weak.

Inuit children were well cared for, treated lovingly and seldom scolded. So that they would have the skills necessary for survival, children were taught by

Game of chance using carved ivory pieces

Sewing a garment as child looks on

their parents when they were around eight. Girls learned to set traps, trim the lamp wick, and make and care for clothing. Boys learned to build a snow house, identify animal tracks, imitate hunting calls and use weapons. Both boys and girls had to know how to handle a sledge and dog team.

During the long winter, Inuit families spent much of their time together indoors. To pass the hours they played games and told stories that passed the history of their people from generation to generation. Some stories were true, others were legends.

The Inuit loved all games but especially games of chance. They made dice from bone. One gambling game used pieces of seal flipper bones carved in the shapes of animals or people. These were dropped one by one over a fur mat; the player having the

**Catching the hair skull
(similar to the game of cup and ball)**

most pieces standing upright would be the winner.

One of the oldest games played all over the world, cat's cradle, was a favourite of the people of the ice. A player wound a long cord of twisted sinew around the fingers of both hands to make shapes resembling animals, *igloo*s and other objects.

When spring came, games moved outdoors.

Summer games drum competition

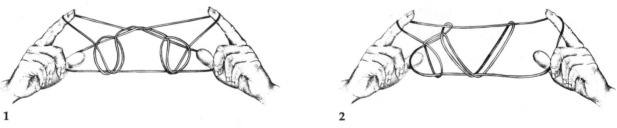

1   2

Cat's Cradle designs: 1/hill and ponds; 2/hare

Children tossed a rabbit skull into the air and tried to spear it with a piece of bone. Games were played using balls made of sealskin stuffed with moss. After the hunt everyone gathered to watch and cheer as the men wrestled, raced and competed in tests of strength.

Visiting and being visited brought much happiness to the Inuit. The most social time of all

Copper Inuit dance dress worn by both men and women

was when fall hunting and fishing had ended and the ice was not yet suitable for seal hunting. In some parts of the Arctic, social life centred around a "dance (or singing) house." There everyone gathered to talk, feast and share religious ceremonies. To the beat of a drum, the people danced and sang. Certain songs were inherited, but only by men. Their songs were their own and no one else could sing them. Women joined in with a chorus, repeating the same words, like a chant. Both men and women composed and sang songs about everyday events and wrote poems for reciting. Sometimes people acted out songs, especially those that told of exciting events. The Inuit sometimes sang while they worked and often poked fun at one another in their songs.

Clothing

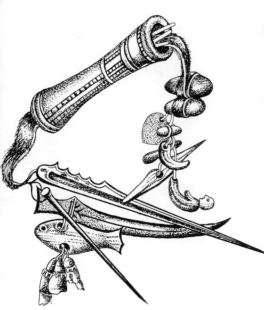

Ivory needle case

Ulu

Scraping hide

In the severe climate of the Arctic, every piece of clothing had to be made by hand with great care. One improperly sewn seam on a garment could mean death for the wearer.

Inuit women learned to sew in childhood, and became highly skilled. When they married they took with them two of their most prized possessions: their *ulus* — crescent-shaped bone knives used for scraping hides — and their sewing kits. Their needles, made of ivory or the hard wing or leg bones of birds, were often kept in small, beautifully decorated tubes.

Sinews from the caribou's back and legs served as thread. These were dried and beaten until the fibres loosened and separated, then were cleaned. Before being sewn, the sinews were soaked in a small bowl.

Although the hides and furs of different animals were used, most garments were made of caribou because of its lightness and warmth. The best skins were taken in the fall hunt when the caribou's hair was short and strong. The Inuit killed only the number of animals needed to outfit their families.

Preparing the animal hides and sewing materials took many hours. The women scraped and cleaned the skins, and later chewed and rubbed them until they were soft and pliable.

A skilled seamstress could take measurements just by looking at a person; she cut the skins according to patterns that had passed from mother

Stone skin scraper

to daughter for centuries. The pieces of hide were then carefully sewn together using a special tight ''lockstitch.'' As the wet sinews dried and shrank, the garment's seams became watertight.

It took about twelve caribou skins to make a complete set of winter clothing for an adult: two pairs of pants and two parkas. The outer set was worn with the fur outside and the inner set with the fur next to the skin.

Although designs differed in some areas of the Arctic, garments were basically the same. They were loose fitting so that air could circulate between layers to provide insulation for added warmth and to prevent sweating. Both men and women wore trousers and parkas. Men's trousers, which were sometimes of polar bear fur, hung below the knees and were tied around the waist with a thong. Women wore two sets: one like the men's and the other like a pair of shorts made of the soft fur of the caribou's belly. The men's parkas had small hoods; the women's hoods were large, reaching to the middle of their backs. Babies, dressed in suits of the finest fawn skin, were carried in their mother's hoods as long as they were nursing, usually until they were two. When inside the hood, babies were bare-legged, and soft, absorbent sphagnum moss took the place of a diaper. A belt tied around the mother's waist held both hood and baby in place. In some parts of the Arctic, parkas had long decorated tailpieces, both front and back.

All parkas were tight at the neck and shoulders and had drawstrings around the sleeves and bottom to prevent warm air from escaping. Hoods were

Woman carrying child

1 **Iglulik man's winter clothing made entirely of caribou skins**
2 **One example of women's summer clothing**
3 **An example of caribou skin dress**

usually trimmed with long fur. The hairs shed snow and water and blew over the face to protect the wearer from sharp winds. Mitts were of sealskin or polar bear fur.

1   2   3

Snow goggles

Stockings made of caribou skin or hare fur fitted over the knees and were tied with thongs. Bird skin slippers were worn with the feathered side next to the foot over the stockings. Warm, flexible waterproof boots were made of sealskin with soles of walrus or bearded seal hide. If slippers were not worn, moss or dried grass was used to line the boots.

To protect the eyes, snow goggles made of narrow pieces of wood or ivory, fitting close to the face above the cheekbones and under the eyebrows, were carved for every member of the family. Narrow slits permitted the wearer to see but reduced the sun's glare and prevented snow blindness.

Every Inuit garment was well shaped for the wearer and beautifully stitched. In some parts of the Arctic red ochre was used to colour the different shades of hide and fur. Animal teeth were sometimes attached as ornaments, or used to make ornate collars and necklaces. For special ceremonies, the women chose the softest pieces of hide to make headbands and collected feathers which were worn in their hair.

Care of clothing did not end when it was made. Snow and ice had to be removed from outer clothing before coming indoors. At the end of each day, every inch of every piece of clothing and footgear had to be checked for wear and damage. No matter how tired a wife might be, she had to make repairs while the clothing was still wet, so that seams would again be watertight by morning. When visiting hunters stayed overnight, the hostess checked and repaired all their outer wear, too, just as she did her husband's.

Housing

BUILDING THE IGLOO

1 Cutting the snow blocks horizontally.

2 The blocks are pried upright using the snow knife.

3 After the circle is marked, the first blocks are placed around it.

4 When the first row of blocks is in position, inclining inwards, the top is cut in a spiral shape.

5 Onto this spiral base the builder adds more blocks, using smaller ones towards the top of the dome. He positions them with the snow knife and punches them into place with his fist for a snug fit. Once the dome is complete, he cuts the doorway to let himself out.

6 The outside of the blocks are shaped to fill in the cracks.

7 Building the entrance-way: only the first two rows of blocks are attached to the main dome.

8 Finished igloo.

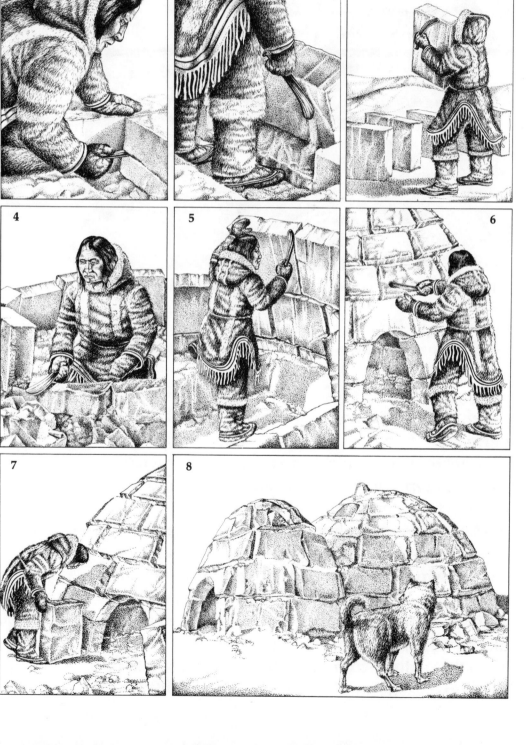

Igloo interior: man using bow drill; woman mending garment

Because of their nomadic life, the Inuit had no permanent homes. Instead, they had a variety of shelters that were quickly and easily constructed, solid enough to withstand severe weather and warm enough for a newborn child.

The Inuit's winter home was the *igloo*, a dome of blocks made from a special kind of wind-packed snow. Using a saw-toothed antler, the builder cut rectangular blocks and laid them on top of each other in a spiral. A sunken floor was created as the blocks were removed.

So that a dome formed as the builder worked upwards, each snow block was sloped slightly

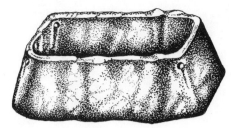

Soapstone pot

Large soapstone lamp with separate compartment for heating blubber

Soapstone lamp stand

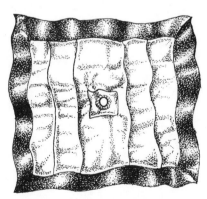

Windowpane of stretched gut

Ivory snow knife

inwards. It was then trimmed with an ivory knife, and punched into place with the fist for a snug fit. The last block had a hole for ventilation, like a jack-o'-lantern top. Loose snow was packed into crevices to make the *igloo* windtight. Sometimes the builder added a window made of ice or semi-transparent seal intestine into which he cut a small peephole.

The Inuit had no furniture. Snow platforms were left on three sides of the *igloo* as it was being built: one for the family bed, and two smaller ones for sitting, cooking or working on. If tent poles were available, they were laid on top of the sleeping platform to keep the furs used as bed covers from touching the snow and becoming wet.

Skins used for the family tent in summer were hung up inside the *igloo*, across the ceiling and down the walls as far as the sleeping platform. They were fastened by leather thongs passed through small holes drilled in the snow blocks and tied outside the *igloo* to bone or wooden crosspieces. The space between the tent cover and the igloo helped keep out the cold.

Because there is little wood in the Arctic, the Inuit did not have ordinary fires. Instead, for both heat and light, a lamp was placed in the centre of the *igloo*. A bowl in the shape of a half-moon was carved from soapstone (a soft, slippery-feeling rock), and in it a wick of hair or dried moss burned the blubber or fat which served as fuel. Fire was made by striking pieces of pyrite ("fool's gold") together or by rotating a fire drill with a leather thong and catching the sparks in grass or willow catkins. Around the lamp was built a framework of poles that could hold wet clothes and pots for cooking and melting snow.

A short, usually low tunnel through which people crawled was added as an entrance to the *igloo*. This served as a windbreak and helped keep the warmth in the main living area. Sometimes smaller side domes were added as storerooms or shelters for the dogs.

Groups of families settling together at winter hunting grounds often joined *igloo*s together with tunnels. They could then visit one another without going outdoors.

Although the lamps were adjusted to give just the right amount of heat and light, after some time the insides of the *igloos* would become very dark from the lamps' constant smoking. When this happened, the family simply built another *igloo*.

In the spring, the lower part of Inuit houses was often made of snow and the upper part of skins. Summer housing was simpler, since tents were made using sealskin or caribou. The shape of these shelters varied: eastern Inuit hung their skins from a central ridgepole; those of the west hung theirs from a standing pole to make a cone-shaped dwelling. In the treed area of the Mackenzie River Delta, families built wooden houses set partly into the ground.

At one time the people of both the eastern Arctic and the flat barrens of central Canada constructed stone houses, but these disappeared long before the Europeans arrived. Houses were also sometimes made of whalebone covered with sod. Wherever the Inuit went, they built their shelters of the materials at hand, making the best out of very little.

Food

Meat and blubber were the basic foods of the Inuit diet. In such a cold climate, fat was as important as meat. Without it, people could not survive.

The Inuit spent little time cooking. Meat from a freshly killed walrus or seal would be immediately cut into pieces and eaten raw while it was still warm and tasted good. Raw meat was much harder to digest but provided valuable nutrients. The raw skin of the white whale and the narwhal contained as much vitamin C as oranges, and helped prevent illnesses such as scurvy. The Inuit were especially fond of raw seal liver, and this, too, provided many vitamins, especially A and D.

Meat taken to the *igloo* was cut into pieces and put in a pot made from a hollowed-out stone, or into a waterproof vessel of walrus hide. Sometimes meat was cooked over the lamp-fire by adding hot stones to water, but this took a long time and the result was

Family eating around soapstone lamp and pot

Prong for carrying blubber, which was often eaten with fresh berries

Sieve for separating snow from autumn berries

Hide berry-collecting bag with scraper attached

Food drying rack

not very appetizing. The family ate sitting in a circle around the pot. Using his knife or a bone fork, the father speared the first piece of meat and held it between his teeth, cutting some off close to his lips. The knife and the chunk of meat were passed around the circle, each person cutting in turn. Even five-year-olds were trusted with the knife.

Fish provided variety to the Inuit's diet. They also enjoyed blood soup, partly digested willow buds and twigs from the gizzards and intestines of ptarmigans, partly digested seaweed from the innards of various sea animals, and seal intestines and stomachs stuffed with partly digested shrimp.

Although meat was preserved by freezing and salmon by drying, continual hunting was necessary. Successful hunting depended upon the weather and the availability of game, and often neither was good. Sometimes the people enjoyed great feasts, sometimes they endured famine. Whole villages might die of starvation. And without fat to fuel their lamps, they could freeze to death.

In summer, food was more easily obtained. The Inuit ate vetch roots, sorrel leaves, rosewood stems and seaweed as well as different berries. In early summer they collected the eggs of wild birds, being careful to leave enough for hatching.

Children enjoyed a treat made from whipped blubber and cloudberries.

All drinking water was melted snow or ice. Sometimes even sea ice was drunk. When water remains frozen for several years it is no longer salty.

Hunting and Fishing

Because their lives depended upon them, the Inuit greatly respected all animals. The wildlife of the Arctic provided not only food but also materials for heat, light, transportation, clothing, shelter, tools, weapons and many other essentials.

Survival depended upon a man's hunting skill. No meat meant not only no food but also no fat. No fat meant no light or heat and — most important of all — no water. Without food and a means to melt snow, the Inuit faced death.

Each time he hunted, a man pitted himself against the animals and the elements. There were no weather forecasts then; he "read" the sky and set out, knowing he might never return. There were no signposts to tell him where he was. He might become lost in a blizzard or stranded on an ice floe. The animal he hunted with only a bow and arrow might weigh many times more than he did. Every hunt required great strength, courage and skill.

Out of driftwood, bone, antler and pieces of hide, the Inuit made bows and arrows, harpoons, spears, bird darts, traps and snares.

Their most important weapon was the harpoon. Its length, weight and design depended upon where and how it was used and the size of the sea animal being hunted. Most harpoon heads separated from the shaft as the animal was struck. Sealskin lines attached to both shaft and head were held by the hunter so that he would not lose either his shaft or his catch. To anchor an animal after a hit, the hunter could plunge his shaft into the ice, or — when seal hunting through *agloo*s — throw it across the hole. On sea hunts men tied inflated sealskin floats to

Caribou hunters; inukshuks in background

their harpoon lines. When a wounded animal dove underwater, the floats acted as a drag, pulling the animal up to the surface where it could be killed with spears.

The seal provided many of the Inuit's needs: meat and fat for nourishment, oil for lamps and heat, and skin for clothing and boots. In winter the Inuit lived where the seal hunting was best, near fairly deep water covered by an even layer of ice, or in areas where the ice was broken by tides and currents.

Seal hunting required great patience. Helped by their dogs, hunters first searched for *agloo*s, the holes to which the seals had to come for air. These *agloo*s were like tiny molehills with a 2½-centimetre- (1-inch-)wide hole at the top, covered with rime which formed as the seal's breath froze. The hunter carefully scraped away the rime to examine the larger hole beneath, so that he could see the direction from which the seal would approach the surface. He then lowered into the hole a piece of bird's down tied to a thread, and remoulded the *agloo*. The slightest movement of the feather would

Hunting with bow and arrow

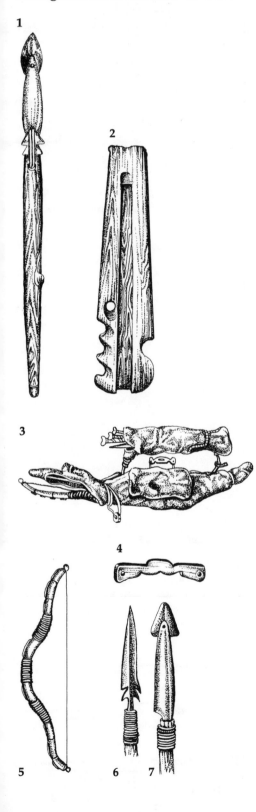

1/Lance; 2/Throwing board, held between hand and weapon, for added thrust; 3/Sealskin carrying case for bow and arrows; 4/Ivory handle for bow case; 5/Bow having splinted staves; 6/Solid antler arrowhead; 7/Arrow having flint blade and antler foreshaft

Ice scoop of musk ox horn

Agloo probe made of antler

tell the hunter that the seal had arrived.

Sometimes it was a long wait. Seals have many breathing holes, and it might be hours — or even days — before a seal came to the hole where the hunter waited. During that time he had to stand or sit perfectly still, ready at any moment to plunge his harpoon downwards with all his strength. In severe weather he would build a windbreak of snow blocks in the same way he built an *igloo*.

In the spring, seals enlarged their breathing holes and pulled themselves onto the ice to bask in the sun. The hunters stole up on them by pretending to be seals, slithering across the ice on their stomachs. A hunter might take one to two hours to get within harpooning distance. Moving like this when the ice was covered with meltwater was a real test of the hunter's hardiness and endurance.

Large sea mammals were hunted from *kayak*s or from the edge of ice floes. Hunters had to be able to throw their harpoons over 6 metres (20 feet) and be strong enough to anchor a struggling 800-kilogram (2,000-pound) walrus until it could be killed with spears. *Kayak* hunters threaded lines through the skin of the dead animal to tow it ashore with several *kayak*s working in tandem. A lone hunter could use inflated sealskins to help him float his catch home. Carcasses were skinned and quartered quickly after death, before they froze. During a hunt, an animal belonged to the first person who saw it, no matter who killed it, but the meat was shared by all.

Caribou were hunted for food, but especially for skins. It was difficult to get close to the herds because the land was bare. So the hunters

Seal indicator made from down

Flensing knife, to strip blubber or skin

Jigging for fish with line and hook

sometimes erected *inukshuk*s — piles of stones that, like scarecrows, resembled human forms. These could frighten the caribou into running towards river fords where the hunters waited in *kayak*s. At other times, women and children helped by sneaking up behind a herd, then jumping up and shrieking and waving their arms, frightening the animals into a specially built corridor of poles. The caribou became trapped and could be killed easily by

Dog guiding the way to an agloo

1 & 2/Ivory plugs used for closing carcass wounds; 3/Throat plug, used to keep air in seal's lungs for easy towing of carcass; 4/Jig with hook; 5/Hook and sinker; 6/Stringer

1

2

3

Hunting seal at edge of an ice floe, with harpoon rack in foreground

Harpoon shaft and head

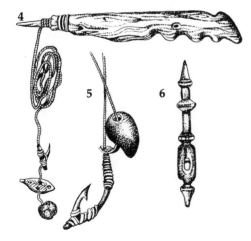

4

5   6

the waiting men.

Caribou were rarely hunted in midwinter, when their meat was too lean and their fur too thick. But if winter hunting were necessary, the Inuit lured the caribou into snow pits by the smell of human urine, which attracted animals because it was salty.

The Inuit caught fish with fishlines, spears and later nets. They lay on the ice on a mat of driftwood or twigs to fish for salmon. No bait was needed. From one hand the fisherman suspended two ivory jigs (lures) which he moved to attract the fish, while his other hand held a three-pronged spear with a 2-metre (7-foot) seal thong attached, ready to strike.

In the central Arctic, stone barriers were placed across rivers to catch char as they came upstream. Two walls were placed a short distance from one another; one was partly open, the other closed. When the char reached the closed wall, the fisherman dropped a rock into the gap in the one behind them, trapping the fish for easy spearing.

Sometimes men formed a line across a stream so that many fish could be caught during a "run" (when fish moved upstream to spawn). In a few areas, Inuit made traps of braided dwarf willow.

An *Inuk* (Inuit person) never hunted for sport: he believed that all animals had souls and that man could kill only in order to live, so he treated all of them with great respect. If he did not, the animal's soul would be angry and hunting would be bad. This applied to fishing as well. The fisherman believed that if he laid his catch in a circle around him with their heads pointing towards the water he would always be in the centre of a school of fish.

On the Move

Travelling from one hunting area to another meant that the Inuit had no permanent home. As well as hunting boats they needed safe and sturdy transportation to carry their families and belongings over long distances.

The main hunting craft was the *kayak*, a slender, light boat for one person that moved silently in the water and was easy to handle and carry. It was from 3½ to 6½ metres (12 to 22 feet) long and was totally enclosed except for a central cockpit where the hunter sat covered with a waterproof cape of gut. During a hunt, the *kayak* might turn upside down in the water and then be righted by the hunter's skillful use of his double-bladed paddle. Hunting gear and sealskin floats were fastened to the *kayak* deck with thongs tied to bone or ivory buttons or knobs.

The men built the framework of the *kayak* using arched rib bones or pieces of driftwood lashed together with sinew or gut. Covers of caribou hide, walrus hide or sealskin were carefully stretched over the frame and sewn together by the women using their lockstitch. When the *kayak* was ready, its skin would be tight as a drum and able to withstand the roughest seas.

The *umiak* was a large open boat, 9 to 12 metres (30 to 40 feet) long, which could carry many people. It was needed for both whaling and transporting families and all their goods. The same materials were used in its construction as for *kayaks* except that the pieces of wood were larger and heavier. The hide cover was tied to the inside of the craft with thongs. Sometimes a sail, made from seal intestines, was added.

1/Umiak; 2/Mouthpiece for inflating bladder float; 3/Button for kayak strap; 4/Seal hide float; 5/Wearing board to support resting paddle; 6/Kayak; 7/Scraper for removing ice from kayak surface; 8/Harpoon line coiling stand; 9/Towing float; 10/Ivory towing device; 11/Implement for cleaning umiak between woodwork and skins

Sealskin kayak jacket and buckle

When families were on the move, the *umiak* was rowed by the women and usually steered with a paddle by a man at the stern. Other men travelled alongside or behind in kayaks.

In the winter, travel was mainly by dog sledge. The sledge was 4½ to 9 metres (15 to 30 feet) long, depending upon its use. It was made of two runners joined by crossbars. When wood was not available, the frame was made of whalebone, ivory, horn or baleen (a stiff substance from the jaw of a whale), or even from frozen fish or hides. Runners were narrow at the back and wide and curved up in front, and were "shoed" with whalebone. In some parts of

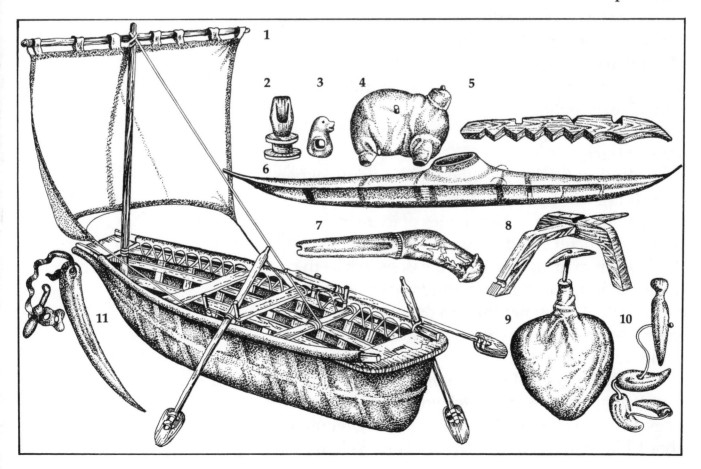

the Arctic, caribou antlers from which the points had been removed were fixed to the back of the sledge to help the driver hold on and steer.

Crossbars were lashed to the runners in such a way that the sledge could bend slightly as it went over rough ground. To make it slide better, a paste of mud or peat mould (dug from under the snow) was packed on the runners and iced with water. Bumps and large cracks in the ice made the sledge tip easily even when carefully loaded and handled.

It took six to twelve dogs to pull a loaded sledge, with the strongest dogs in front. Harnesses and traces were made of sealskin or caribou thongs. In the west and below the timberline, where trails were narrow, dogs were harnessed in pairs or in single file. But in the rough, open spaces of the north, each dog was harnessed on a separate trace and could find its own footing. Traces were gathered in a fan-shaped arrangement, the lead dog on the longest trace.

The best and safest travelling was in winter when everything was frozen. In spring, when the snow began to melt, thin, jagged edges of ice made walking difficult and damaged the dogs' paws, so the women made footgear for the dogs just as they did for their family, checking and repairing them each night. Sometimes the ice edges were so sharp that the sealskin boots wore out faster than a woman could make them.

Because he depended upon their strength and stamina, a hunter had to catch enough food for his dogs as well as his family. A working dog required about 1 kilogram (1 pound) of meat and ⅛ kilogram

Sealskin harness. Fastener allows dog
to be released from main trace

1/Device for fastening dog traces to
main trace; 2/Fastener

1

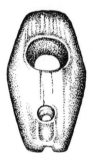

2

(¼ pound) of fat a day, although sometimes dogs
went for several days without food and were still
able to pull.

However he travelled, an *Inuk* had to be totally in
tune with his surroundings. His knowledge of
winds and weather, water currents and tides, and
the behaviour and migratory patterns of animals
and birds might make the difference between life
and death. He had to make allowances for unusual
conditions. When the Arctic sky is overcast, low and
bright, it can merge with the snow-covered land into
one endless, even whiteness. In such a "whiteout,"
a tiny nearby lemming can appear to be a distant
giant musk ox.

Mirages are as common in the Arctic as in the
desert. They are caused by the bending of light rays
between layers of air that are of different
temperatures. Distant objects not only change shape
and size but also move. People, mountains and
islands can seem so real that a traveller will change
course to meet or avoid them, only to discover that
they have shifted, shimmered and finally
disappeared, having never been there at all.

An *Inuk* could tell what lay ahead and how far he
had to go by "reading" the sky, which reflected the
colours of the land and sea below. A hunter
travelling by sledge across the sea ice knew he
would reach open water where dull grey cloud
appeared on the horizon. When he saw a white glare
in the sky, he knew that he would have icefields or a
large, snow-covered expanse to cross.

In a storm or whiteout a hunter could tell his
direction of travel by using his knowledge of local

Inukshuk or landmark

winds and examining the angle of the wind-sculpted snow ridges. He also looked for stone cairns, or *inukshuk*s. Distances were measured not in kilometres or miles but in "sleeps" — the number of nights required to cover the distance.

With the warming spring, the ice that covers the sea begins melting. The currents, tides and winds shift and crack the ice, pushing it into ridges or breaking it apart, making wide channels and lakes of open water. At the floe edge where the land ice ends, visibility is obscured by rolling, dark grey clouds of steam as the warmer sea meets the cold air. This was a time of special danger for the hunter, when he might be crushed, or left stranded on a floe that had floated away, with no means of returning to the land.

Beliefs and Customs

To the Inuit, the supernatural was as normal as the natural, everyday world in which they lived. They believed in a special power or force "up there," and that there were spirits who sometimes helped people and sometimes tricked them. One spirit was a woman who lived on the sea bottom, where the sins of man were said to settle in her hair like dirt. If she were made angry, there would be poor hunting because she would keep the sea animals away from the land.

The Inuit believed everything had a soul, and when a person or animal died the spirit could enter another living creature. A hunter might place his harpoon beside the lamp the first night after a kill so that the animal's soul — believed to be still in the harpoon head — could warm itself by the flame. Festivals were sometimes held to honour the animals that had been killed, and special rituals were carried out to ensure good hunting in the future.

There were many Inuit taboos. Land and sea animals could not be handled together in any way, so eating caribou and walrus meat on the same day was forbidden. Weapons that had been used for hunting land animals had to be smoked over a fire of seaweed before being used for hunting seal. Clothing of caribou hides was not sewn while seals were being hunted.

As safeguards against evil, the Inuit wore a variety of amulets (religious charms): owl claws to give strong hands; caribou ears for quick hearing; a willow branch for growth. A fish skin was placed with a fisherman's tools to bring good luck, and a loon skin was sewn into the side of a *kayak* to give good speed. Sometimes amulets were hung or offerings left around a stone in places where travellers would encounter dangerous conditions.

Shamans were people — usually men — who could talk to the spirits and would receive answers to important questions through solitude and fasting. Shamans had the power to fight angry spirits and to find the guilty person when something wrong had been done. They were usually respected and sometimes feared, although they lived, dressed and hunted like everyone else in the community.

People who were ill and women ready to give birth were separated from the rest of the family. A woman often delivered her child alone and remained alone with her baby in a separate house or tent for about a month. She could not eat certain foods and was not allowed to go visiting. The navel cord of the baby was bitten off or cut with a stone knife or mussel shell and kept as an amulet.

When someone died, the body was usually wrapped in skins and laid on the tundra or in the hills, within a ring of stones. Weapons and tools were placed beside the body. Because the power of death was believed to be the greatest of all powers, it was the most feared. In some cases the family of the dead one bathed themselves and thoroughly cleaned their homes. Those who attended the corpse threw away the clothes they had worn and put on new ones.

When a child was born it was usually given the name of a dead relative. It was believed that the soul of the dead person entered into the child and guided

1/Amulet: feet of horned owl; 2/Young girl's amulet worn to ensure male children; 3/Shaman's equipment and Alaskan Inuit death mask; 4/ Labrador man's tattoo design; 5/Baffin man's tattoo; 6/Caribou woman's tattoo

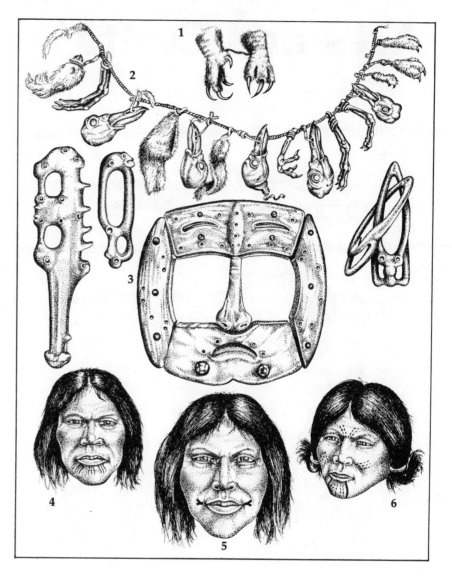

him in his early years.

Tattooing was known to all Inuit but was generally seen on women. Designs were made on the chin, forehead, cheeks, arms, breasts and thighs, either by pulling a soot-covered thread through the skin or by pricking the skin with a needle dipped in a mixture of soot and seaweed. Women without proper tattoos were said to go to an unhappy place after death: "the land of the crestfallen."

Some men wore labrets: pieces of ivory inserted in the skin at the corners of the mouth or under the lower lip.

42

Arts and Crafts

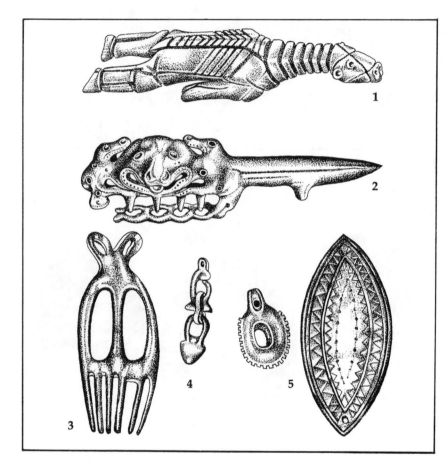

1/Ivory carving of swimming polar bear (skeleton motif) by Dorset people; 2/Stylized ivory carving of bear; 3/Woman's ivory comb; 4/Ivory chain links; 5/Ivory pendants;

The Inuit have been skilled craftspeople for centuries. Using their hands and the materials around them, they not only designed and made all the items needed for everyday life but they also decorated them, using pieces of ivory, light and dark skins, stencilled or dyed leather trimmings and bone beads. They made pottery, carved faces on rocky outcroppings, painted wooden masks used in religious ceremonies, and strung fox and seal teeth for necklaces.

Women fashioned bags from unusual materials like fish heads, and in the eastern Arctic made coiled

Grooving knife

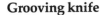

Whittling knife

baskets from long grasses, weaving strips of sealskin and whale sinew between rows.

The Inuit invented the *igloo* and the *kayak*, and have been called the world's first tailors because of their expert garment making.

Carving was an everyday skill, since bowls, tools, arrowheads and spearheads were always needed. The carvers discovered that soapstone was ideal for making cooking pots because it could take heat well and baked to a glossy hardness when it became really hot. Damaged soapstone pots were mended with a cement made of blood, clay and dog hair, and then were heated over a flame until the mend set. Ivory was best for carving items that needed to be strong, like harpoon heads and snow knives.

Sometimes — especially during the long winter months — the Inuit carved shapes of animals or people purely for pleasure. But a carver did not just pick up a stone and begin to work on it. He held it, thought about it and felt it all over. The Inuit believed there was an image within each stone that would be freed when it was carved, that its soul would be released. In this, as in all other aspects of Inuit life, there was harmony between man and nature.

The Inuit art forms were simple but strong and full of imagination. They showed scenes of everyday life, often reflecting ancient myths and traditions. Among recently found artifacts carved thousands of years ago are tiny, delicate figures made of bone, stone, ivory and driftwood. Some are smaller than 2½ centimetres (an inch) high, yet they are remarkable works of art.

The Coming of the White People

With the coming of the white man, the centuries-old ways of the Inuit began to change. Explorers, whalers, traders, missionaries and government officials brought new ideas, tools, weapons, religion, education and laws to the North which altered the Inuit's lives.

It is believed that the first white people seen by the Inuit were the Norsemen, about A.D. 1003. Several hundred years later, scattered groups of Inuit met and traded with European explorers for goods like knives and iron pots.

But it was the English, Scottish and American whalers during the seventeenth and eighteenth centuries who seriously affected the age-old values of this ancient people. The Inuit had worked only for their families. Now they worked for whalers — not only on ships and at processing stations but also farther inland trapping animals — to supply furs, oil and other whale products for far-off markets. They no longer had to hunt for food; whalers gave it to them in exchange for fox pelts.

Then white men came to live in the Arctic. Anglican and Roman Catholic missionaries brought Christianity to the North in the 1850s, devised a system of writing, and established schools, hospitals and nursing stations. Trading posts were built all across the Arctic by the men of the Hudson's Bay Company. These gave the Inuit easy access to manufactured goods, especially guns. Animals could be killed easier and faster, and their numbers decreased. People could not live off the land as they had in the past. The Inuit moved close to the posts and became dependent on the white man's food.

Some found jobs, but for many there was nothing to replace the old way of life.

The Inuit had no resistance to the white man's diseases, and thousands died. Within two generations of contact with the whites, ninety per cent of the people of the Mackenzie River Delta had died. In Labrador there were 3,000 Inuit in 1750; by 1946, only 750 remained.

World War II brought modern technology to the Arctic. A number of Inuit found jobs at air bases and weather stations that were set up for the defence of North America.

Seeing the impact of the white man upon life in the Arctic, James Houston, an artist and friend of the Inuit, began in 1949 to think about ways they could earn a living using their traditional skills. He helped them sell their carvings in southern Canada, and later encouraged them to make prints and other art forms.

The West Baffin Eskimo Co-operative was the first of several co-operatives (groups of people working together) organized to promote this new and important industry. Before long, copperplate engravings, printed fabrics and ceramics were added to the selection of carvings and block and stencil prints.

The names of several artists, carvers and printmakers have become well known, and some — like Kenojuak and Pitseolak — have been honoured by the government of Canada. Inuit works of art now command high prices in specialty shops and galleries in many parts of the world.

Today, Inuit serve on town councils, on the

Northwest Territories Council and in the Canadian parliament. They have formed Inuit organizations to protect their political rights and their culture, and are negotiating with the federal government for their land rights. Co-operatives have been formed not only for artistic works but also for industries like char fishing, fur garment making, tourism and sport hunting. The Inuit want to manage their own affairs and control their land and its natural resources.

Most Inuit families now live in conventional houses, shop for their food and clothing, enjoy television, and travel by plane and snowmobile. They have found new ways of surviving in the Arctic. Some of the old ways remain, though there is no turning back — the lives of the people of the ice have changed forever.

Glossary

agloo - seal's breathing hole in the ice

aurora borealis - ribbons or arches of moving, coloured light. Caused when electrically charged particles from the sun collide with particles of oxygen and nitrogen in the earth's atmosphere

cloudberries - orange-yellow berries like raspberries, sometimes called "baked apple"

igdlo - "house" in the Inuit language

igloo - a dome-shaped house made of snow blocks

Inuk - an Inuit person

inukshuk - a pile of stones shaped like a human form

Inuktitut - the Inuit language

kayak - a long, narrow hide boat for one person, used for hunting

lichen - a mosslike plant without flowers which grows in patches on the ground, rocks and trees

lockstitch - a sewing stitch that locks two threads together at small intervals

permafrost - permanently frozen earth

pyrite - a brass-yellow mineral containing sulphur and iron

rime - a covering of ice crystals formed on objects by fog or water vapour that has frozen

sorrel - a sour-juiced, acid-leaved herb

ulu - a crescent-shaped bone knife used for scraping hides

umiak - a large open boat used for whaling and transporting families and their belongings

vetch - a climbing herb belonging to the pea family